A Little Book of Friendship

Published in Nashville, Tennessee, by Thomas Nelson, Inc., Publishers, and distributed in Canada by Word Communications, Ltd., Richmond, British Columbia.

Printed in Singapore

Library of Congress Cataloging-in-Publication Data

Caswell, Helen Rayburn.
   A little book of friendship / Helen Caswell.
      p.   cm.
   ISBN 0-7852-8033-2
   1. Friendship—Juvenile literature. [1. Friendship.] I. Title.
BF575.F66C37 1995
177'.6—dc20   94-24373
                                                                     CIP
                                                                    AC

2 3 4 5 6 — 00 99 98 97 96

A Little Book of Friendship

Helen Caswell

OLIVER NELSON

THOMAS NELSON PUBLISHERS

Nashville • Atlanta • London • Vancouver

Friends are the ones
who love you
no matter what
you do. But if
you want to
have a friend,
you have to
be one,
too.

Sometimes
it's hard
to make new friends
but you should
always try.

When people
don't seem friendly
sometimes
they're only
shy.

A smile's
the thing
for making
friends —
much better
than a
pout.

And you can
give your
smiles away
for years
and not
run out.

You like to
do things
for a friend,
and they
do things
for you.

And work that's
hard for only
one
     is easier
  with two.

It's nice
to have a
special place
but sometimes,
with just
one—

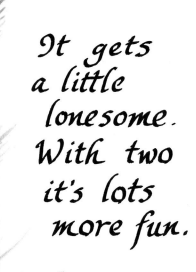

It gets
a little
lonesome.
With two
it's lots
more fun.

And if you find
some goodies
that no one knows
are there—

You'll feel
a whole lot better
if you find
a friend
and share.

Some friends are young
and some
are old;
some have
four feet
and furry
faces.

There are friends
at church and
friends at school—
all sorts of
friends
in lots
of places.

Best of all my friends
is One
that I can talk to
when I pray.
I never see Him
but I know
He's close
beside me
every day.